A killi kinky cottage

The murder of Maxwell Garvie

Murder World

Scotland

Book 1

Murder World: Real crimes, real killers.

Table of Contents

Introduction 4

Prologue 6

Chapter 1: The Ideal Couple 9

Chapter 2: Swinging..18

Chapter 3: Max and Trudy and Sheila and Brian.............28

Chapter 4: Max Goes Missing..............................38

Chapter 5: The Trial 46

Chapter 6: Aftermath...55

Conclusion..61

About the Author..64

Other Murder World Scotland Books 65

Introduction

There's no art to find the mind's construction in the face.

Macbeth, Act I, Scene IV, by William Shakespeare

I was born and brought up in the North East of Scotland, and I can clearly remember hearing my parents talking in hushed voices about some people I didn't know called Max and Sheila Garvie and Brian Tevendale. Like any sensible nine-year old, I knew that the use of hushed voices implied that they were talking about something deeply interesting. Something that they didn't feel was appropriate for my sensitive young ears. A surreptitious scan of the front page of the local newspaper revealed heated discussion of something called a *"kinky cottage."* I knew what a cottage was, but I had no idea what *"kinky"* meant. Except that I was aware of a catchy piece of music called *"kinky boots"*. Assuming that the whole thing had something to do with footwear, I quickly lost interest and went back to studying my Commando War comics.

It wasn't until many, many years later that I finally read the full story of Max and Sheila Garvie and their kinky cottage. In the most basic terms, there is no mystery here. We know who was murdered and who pulled the trigger and we have a reasonable idea of why. What makes this case so fascinating is that the three people involved in the murder all gave very different accounts of what happened.

Depending on who you choose to believe, this could be the story of a fragile woman, traumatized by the incessant and bizarre sexual demands of her overbearing and violent husband, who sought solace in the company of a besotted young man and was then further traumatized and punished when he unexpectedly took bloody revenge on her husband. But, it could also be the story of a ruthless and manipulative woman who used her sexuality to inveigle a naïve young man to commit murder on her behalf and then discarded him when he was of no further use to her. Or, it could be none of these things.

Let's take a look at the fascinating case of the Killing at Kinky Cottage and see if we can make sense of the evidence.

Prologue

The Swinging Sixties never really made it as far as the North East of Scotland. Free love and sexual liberation may have been happening in London, but in the Howe o' the Mearns, things went on much as they ever had. The Howe (the word means "*wide valley*") includes the market town of Laurencekirk and the villages of Aberluthnot, Fettercairn, Fordoun, Arbuthnott and Garvock. The area is prosperous farming land, famous for its fertile red soil and its use of a distinctive dialect, Doric, in which boys are *loons*, girls are *queans* and casual farm workers are *orramen*. Up until the late 1960s, the only reason that most outsiders had heard of the Mearns at all was because it had been used as the setting for *A Scots Quair*, the much-loved trilogy of novels about farming life in the early years of the Twentieth Century by Scots author Lewis Grassic Gibbon.

The town of Laurencekirk, viewed from Garvock Hill

Photo: John Dally

Of course, the people of this area were aware of such things as *"the permissive society"* even if they had little experience of it themselves. The Profumo scandal in 1963 had suggested that even people at the very highest levels of society in London were involved in sexual high-jinks of the sort that could only be alluded to in guarded terms in family newspapers. And those newspapers gleefully told their readers about a potent mix of drugs, alcohol, sex and music and fashion that was sweeping some of Britain largest cities. Popular television programmes such as the Avengers, most of which were still being broadcast in black and white in 1968, were challenging conventions and showing a world where traditional roles were changing. Even in staid, grey Laurencekirk there were whisperings that perhaps there were "*goings-on*" at luxurious West Cairnbeg Farm, home of wealthy local landowner Maxwell Garvie.

It didn't take the people of the area long to start referring to the farm as "*kinky cottage*" and, even if most of them had no more than a dim idea of what went on there, there was a general, tutting and shaking of heads. This wasn't the sort of thing, they said, that we want happening here. When it became apparent much later that events at the farm had led, indirectly, to murder, many people claimed to be unsurprised. It seemed to some of them a short moral and philosophical step from wife swapping to murder. However, if the people of the Mearns were horrified, they were also fascinated in equal measure. Horrified of course that such a thing could happen in a decent, God-fearing place like Laurencekirk. But fascinated too at the prurient details they devoured in sensational reports in the local and national press...

Chapter 1: The Ideal Couple

Maxwell Garvie was fit and broad shouldered with the kind of dark good looks that are sometimes called *"brooding"* by romantic novelists. In 1954, Max was twenty years old and one of the most eligible bachelors in the North East. He wasn't just dashing and handsome, he was also the son and heir of a wealthy Kincardineshire family which owned large tracts of land round the town of Laurencekirk. Max was a farmer, but not of the muddy wellington variety. In England, he would probably have been referred to as a *"gentleman farmer."* In the North-East, he was simply known as someone with enough money not to have to traipse round fields himself, instead controlling the Garvie lands through the offices of a grieve who looked after the day-to-day running of West Cairnbeg, the family farm situated just outside the small town of Laurencekirk.

Max was always known as a *"ladies' man"* and by the time that he was twenty he had already courted and discarded a number of girlfriends. Then, in mid-1954, he attended a local dance where he met Sheila Watson, a shy, slim, elegant blonde. Sheila was just seventeen, but she was bright and vivacious in addition to being stunningly beautiful and Max Garvie was instantly smitten.

Sheila's background was very different to Garvie's. She was the daughter of a stonemason employed on the Queen's estate at Balmoral, a man known for his short temper and strict views on just about everything, a man who viewed any form of pleasure as suspect and saw frugality and restraint as the only praiseworthy human virtues. Her mother too was a woman of inflexible views. When people described Edith Watson they most often used words like *"upright"* and *"forthright"*. Edith may have lacked the puritanical streak of her husband, but like him she valued honesty, integrity and hard work ahead of most other things. All these things are entirely praiseworthy, but they must have produced a stifling home atmosphere for a gregarious and fun-seeking young girl.

Sheila was employed at Balmoral Castle for a short period as a maid, though she longed to escape both from her parent's oversight and from the predictably tedious formal routine of life as a domestic servant in the Queen's retinue at Balmoral. Her opportunity came in 1954 when the Watson family moved to the small fishing town of Stonehaven, on the North Sea coast, just fifteen miles south of Aberdeen and a few miles north of Laurencekirk.

Stonehaven is a fishing village composed of grey granite houses perched on a coastline overlooking the grey North Sea. It wasn't precisely a Mecca for fun and excitement in the 1950s, but it was a distinct improvement over being stuck in remote Balmoral Castle for a young woman in search of a little fun. Sheila found work as a secretary in the town and, just like most other young women of the time, she spent some of her money on clothes, shoes, having her hair done and going to dances, to the bafflement and fury of her father. When she met Max Garvie, Sheila had relatively little experience with men and had never even had a regular boyfriend. To her, Max must have represented everything that her father was not: he was wealthy and lavish in his spending, he wore smart suits, drove fast cars and enjoyed the best restaurants and nightclubs. Unsurprisingly, Sheila was swept off her feet by the constant attention of this very attractive young man.

Stonehaven

Photo: Colin Smith

Max was a young man used to getting his way and he quickly made it clear that he wanted Sheila. Her apparent shyness and nervousness seemed only to make him more determined and more insistent. He pursued Sheila and soon they were engaged. On June 21st, 1955 Sheila Watson and Max Garvie were married in a lavish ceremony which was reported in the society pages of the local press. He was twenty-one and she was just eighteen. They must have seemed like the ideal couple: she, charming, beautiful and demure and he, darkly handsome, wealthy and clearly besotted with his young bride.

After they were married, Sheila and Max moved to live

together in the farmhouse at West Cairnbeg which the Garvie family had owned for more than sixty years. Located less than one mile north of the town of Laurencekirk, the house was far from most people's image of a farmhouse. The five bedroom building had a large conservatory, a massive oak staircase and its own stunning, walled private gardens. It was furnished and decorated to the highest standards and Max Garvie missed no opportunity to show off his home or his new bride. The house became the scene of lavish parties where the great and the good of the Mearns were entertained in some style and West Cairnbeg became the focus of social life in the area.

Photo: Ian Cleland

Despite the fact that Max Garvie was entranced by fast

13

cars and living the high life, he also had a reputation of being a conscientious farmer. Bill Scorgie, the grieve for West Cairnbeg Farm, recalled him as a man who was interested in the land and always looking for ways to make improvements on the farm. This connection with the land brought Garvie the respect of the conservative element in the Mearns – money and smart clothes were all very well, but a man who looked after the land, well, there couldn't be much wrong with him, could there?

While Max looked after the running of the farm, Sheila slipped easily into the role of society hostess. Her clothes came from London, and Max insisted that she dressed to show off her stunning figure. The Garvies became pillars of local society and no social event was complete without the presence of the glamorous couple. In 1956, Sheila gave birth to the Garvie's first child, Wendy. The little girl was followed by a sister, Angela the following year. As the fifties gave way to the sixties, Sheila Garvie looked like a woman who had it all: she was beautiful, she had a handsome, wealthy, attentive husband, a fine house and two healthy children.

However, under the surface, things weren't quite so perfect at West Cairnbeg. At the heart of the trouble was Max's continual sense of dissatisfaction. No matter what he did or how much money he spent, he always seemed to become bored and dissatisfied. Take his cars, for example. He would fixate on a new car that he wanted, talking about it incessantly and producing brochures to show everyone how wonderful it was. Then he'd buy it and for a few weeks, he would talk of nothing else. Proudly he'd show it to his friends and family, cleaning it obsessively and telling everyone who'd listen that this was the very thing he had been looking for. Then, often in no more than a month or two, niggles would creep in. His talk about the new car wouldn't be quite so ecstatic. And then, the next set of brochures would appear...

It didn't seem to matter what Max had, he became bored with it very quickly and his sense of discontentment undermined everything he did. He always seemed to be looking for something new, something different in the hope that it would bring him more than fleeting satisfaction. With his cars and other toys, this hardly mattered. Max was sufficiently wealthy that he could afford to indulge his whims without leaving his family short of money. But it wasn't just material possessions with which Max became bored and dissatisfied.

He became critical of Sheila. Mainly of her appearance, but also of how she looked after him and the children and of how she furnished and maintained the house. Sometimes he was critical of the girls. His eldest daughter Wendy in particular, was turning out to be something of a disappointment to Max. The main problem was her weight. By the time that Wendy went to school, she was undeniably plump. Physical appearance was very important to Max and he nagged Wendy incessantly about the importance of being thin. He complained about it to Sheila too, insisting that his daughter take slimming tablets. But nothing seemed to help Wendy lose weight. Max wanted everything around him to look perfect. And that included his family.

Max's dissatisfaction was made worse by his drinking. He had always enjoyed whisky, and as soon as he returned to the house in the evening, he'd make himself a stiff drink. And another. And then another... By the time that the girls were going to school, Max was getting through four or five bottles of whisky each week. And the more that he drank, the more belligerent and discontented he became.

However, as the post-war boom of the Fifties slid into the excitement of the Sixties, things began to change, not just at West Cairnbeg, but right across Britain.

Chapter 2: Swinging

Sexual intercourse began
In nineteen sixty-three
(which was rather late for me)

Annus Mirabilis, Philip Larkin

The sixties in Britain were a time of enormous change. Some of it was obvious – groups like the Beatles, the Rolling Stones and many others gave voice to a desire for change that would overthrow existing conventions and replace them with something quite different. Fashions like the mini-skirt were daring and challenging and the recreational use of drugs such as marijuana and LSD became much more widespread.

These visible, surface changes were just the tip of the iceberg. More importantly than any change in appearances, attitudes were also changing. Scandals like the Profumo affair and the Suez crisis had undermined confidence in the establishment. There was a growing feeling that those in power weren't just as fallible as anyone else, they were also just as likely to give in to temptation as anyone else too. A new breed of politician replaced the old guard – when

Harold Wilson spoke about the need for Britain to embrace the *"white heat of scientific revolution"* in the sixties he was displaying a grasp of the changing face of the world that a previous generation of politicians simply never had to consider.

Other fundamental attitudes were changing too, especially those involving sex. The birth control pill was legalized in the 60s, as was abortion. Homosexuality was finally de-criminalised in the 1960s and the Divorce Reform Act made it easier and simpler for married couples to split up (and by the end of the decade, almost one in two marriages was ending in divorce).

Definitions of what constituted pornography were changing too. Until the 1959 Lady Chatterley's Lover Trial, any publisher of material with a *"tendency to deprave and corrupt those whose minds are open to such immoral influences"* was liable to find themselves in court. After that, sexuality became a legitimate topic for books, films and even the theatre. On television, new shows such as Coronation Street shocked some viewers by dealing with previously taboo topics such as extra-marital affairs and failed marriages. The term *"permissive society"* began to be used, often disapprovingly, to describe a perception of a new world in which sex was not only freely available to all, but practices which only a short time before would have been dismissed as perversions had somehow become acceptable.

However, this perception was often no more than that. Even in London, often portrayed as the hip centre of the Swinging Sixties, these changes only affected very few people. Free love and uninhibited sex were restricted to a tiny minority, even if the popular press and television made it seem much more widespread. Five hundred miles to the north, very little seemed to be changing in Laurencekirk and Max Garvie became increasingly frustrated. According to what he read in the newspapers and watched on television, the permissive society was changing attitudes all around him. But he could see no sign of it in the Howe o' the Mearns.

Max had always had a very strong sex drive, but just like every other aspect of his life, Max became quickly bored with doing the same thing, time after time. He constantly wanted to try new experiences and he subscribed to a number of "*Men's Magazines*" which provided him with a stream of new ideas to try. Sheila complained to friends that, while magazines about farming and the North-East went straight into the waste bin, Max's collection of pornographic magazines was treasured and often pored over. Generally, Sheila would go along with whatever new thing Max wanted to try, not because she was particularly interested but because she was worn down by his constant nagging and occasional threatening.

Max insisted that Sheila wore the latest mini-skirts and other revealing fashions, often brought direct from Carnaby Street to West Cairnbeg. But no matter how much Sheila went along with what Max wanted, her lack of enthusiasm for what he saw as the new sexual revolution was a disappointment to him. He began to criticize her, to complain that she was cold and *'frigid'* and it wasn't long before he began to seek sexual adventures with new partners and to look for ways to bring the permissive society a little closer to Laurencekirk.

One early attempt involved Max's sudden enthusiasm for erotic photography. Inspired by the magazines that he read, Max decided that he would produce his own erotic shots. He involved a very unwilling Sheila and some of his friends, but it became clear that the local police made little distinction between erotic photographs and pornography. When Max began distributing his photographs, although he was not formally charged, it became clear that if he persisted, the police might take a direct interest. Discouraged, Max began to look for more discreet ways to indulge his taste for the exotic.

In the early sixties, he had a small triangle of trees and bushes planted on farmland close to the house at West Cairnbeg. This wasn't considered odd – the wind in the flat, rolling countryside of the Mearns can flatten crops and destroy buildings. Many farmers plant stands of trees to provide shelter for their fields, livestock and buildings. The planting that Max organized did seem a little unusual in that the triangle of ground protected by the new growth was small and seemed to consist of nothing more than a grassy area. When he was asked why this was, Max was happy to explain – he was setting up a nudist colony at the farm. The sharp intake of breath from the residents of Laurencekirk could be heard echoing round the Mearns.

Nudism, which by the 1960s was more generally known by the term "*naturism*" in the UK, had been popular with small numbers of people in Britain since the 1930s. By the 1960s, popularized by films such as the 1960 offering *The Nudist Story* ("*The Citizen Kane of nudist films*" according to a contemporary review in the Manchester Guardian) and propelled by the new interest in freedom of sexual expression, it gained many new followers. However, although promoted by its fans as a healthy alternative lifestyle (the main nudist magazine in the 1960s was titled "*Health and Efficiency*"), for many people, nudism still had sleazy associations more suited to *Carry On* films than to the sober environs of Laurencekirk.

Max Garvie had become first become interested in naturism when he visited a nudist colony during a family holiday in France and then another during a trip to Corsica. He then insisted that Sheila accompany him to a naturist camp near Edinburgh and a smaller nudist retreat near the town of Alford. Enjoying his time at these nudist centres and undeterred by either local disapproval or the vagaries of the Scottish climate, Max Garvie went ahead and set up a part of his farm as a nudist area. This was never a commercial venture or a formally established nudist camp, it was simply a place where Max and selected friends could relax with a few drinks and without the encumbrance of clothes. Not everyone found the atmosphere relaxing – Max insisted that not only Sheila but his two young daughters attended naked parties in the bushes. Sheila and the girls found this excruciatingly embarrassing, but as ever, Max wore them down with constant nagging until they agreed to go along with it. Wendy, Max's oldest daughter later talked about her reaction to these nudist gatherings:

> "I was forced to strip off. Being fat, I was terribly embarrassed. There were old men sitting watching. We went one time to Corsica, which was warm, but my dad tried to set up a place in Scotland and I remember undressing in the freezing cold."[1]

A number of Max's friends and acquaintances clearly did enjoy his nudist gatherings and it wasn't long before locals began referring to West Cairnbeg Farm as "*Kinky Cottage*."

Max's insistence on Sheila attending his nudist gatherings was just another instance of his browbeating her into co-operating with his sexual proclivities. Sheila became depressed and told friends that Max had threatened her (she later claimed that he once threatened to shoot her) and had become physically violent towards her on more than occasion.

Part of the issue was Max's increasing use of drugs. He was regularly swallowing handfuls of Pro-Plus, a caffeine based stimulant. These tablets, which were and are freely available in the UK, give a short-term energy boost, but they can also cause long-term health issues if the recommended dose (no more than one or two tablets per hour) is exceeded. Max regularly took many more than this, and as a result he often had problems sleeping. Instead of cutting back on the stimulant, he began taking Soneryl, a trade name for Butobarbital, a barbiturate used to treat chronic insomnia. Nowadays, doctors recognise that, if Butobarbital is used for more than two weeks, it can cause physical dependence and it loses its effectiveness as a sleeping aid. It was also strongly recommended that Soneryl should not be taken with alcohol. But Max continued to drink four or five bottles of whisky per week while taking this medication, sometimes simultaneously. No wonder that he was also gobbling Pro-Plus and, it was said, supplementing this with *"pep-pills"*, amphetamine based products that were, until 1964, legal in the UK.

Max Garvie in 1966

Unsurprisingly given his intake of drugs and alcohol, Max Garvie's behaviour became increasingly erratic. His nudist gatherings often descended into alcohol fuelled orgies, with Max insisting that Sheila join in the round of wife-swapping. The birth of a son, Lloyd, in 1964 briefly seemed to bring him down-to-earth and he attempted to bring his drinking and drug consumption under control, but the improvement didn't last long. Sheila's depression intensified until, to her relief, Max found a new hobby on which to focus his considerable energy.

Notes

1 *The Sins of My Mother*. Article in The Scotsman

newspaper based on an interview with Wendy Drew (nee Garvie). http://www.scotsman.com/lifestyle/the-sins-of-my-mother-1-595767

Chapter 3: Max and Trudy and Sheila and Brian

Sometime around 1965, Max became interested in learning to fly. He attained his Private Pilot's License and then, never being a man to do things by halves, he bought himself an aircraft and founded a flying club at Fordoun, around four miles north of Laurencekirk.

Fordoun had been an RAF airfield during World War Two, but by the mid-sixties its four hangers and two runways had fallen into disrepair. Enthused by his new hobby, and keen to have somewhere close to his home where he could fly, Max helped fund work at refurbishing the airfield until, by 1966, it was re-opened for civilian light aircraft.

Max bought himself a German Bölkow Bo 208 Junior, a two-seater aircraft capable of gentle aerobatics, and in 1967 he was instrumental in the founding of the Fordoun Flying Club, a small club based at the airfield. Max seemed to love flying the small aircraft over the Mearns, but his piloting was as erratic as the rest of his life. He became known as someone who would drink before flying, and then use pills to offset the effects of the alcohol. He would *"buzz"* friends if he spotted them from the air, diving low over fields and gardens and even chasing cars if he recognised them. He insisted that Sheila accompany him on flights in the aircraft on several occasions, but she was understandably nervous about his approach to flying. It wasn't long before Max was known locally (and amongst other things) as *"The Flying Farmer."*

A Bölkow Bo 208 Junior

Photo: Alan D R Brown

In Scotland, the sixties also brought a surge in Nationalism. The Scottish National Party (SNP) had been founded in 1934, but had found very little electoral success in its first twenty-five years of existence. Then, in 1961, the party won a significant share of the vote at a by-election in Glasgow

Bridgeton. And in 1962, it did the same in West Lothian. Then, in 1967, Winnie Ewing won the Hamilton by-election to become the first SNP Member of Parliament. Suddenly, the SNP was growing at an unprecedented rate and hundreds of new local SNP organisations were founded. Max Garvie had always been interested in Scottish Nationalism and he became involved in an SNP branch in the Howe o' the Mearns.

There he met a young man called Brian Tevendale. Tevendale was just twenty-one when he first met Max, a slim, diffident young man with dark hair and a neatly trimmed beard. The youngest of three children, Tevendale had been born in nearby Stonehaven. His father was well-known in the area as a former policeman who had gone on to win the Distinguished Conduct Medal while serving as a Commando during World War Two. Brian was brought up in the small fishing village of St Cyrus, a few miles south of Laurencekirk on the North Sea coast, where his family ran the Bush Hotel.

After leaving school, Brian went to Aberdeen where he took a course in wireless operation, intended for people who wanted to follow a career in the merchant marine. Just one year into the course, his father died and Brian abandoned his studies and his plans for a career at sea. Instead, he joined the Army, entering the Medical Corps. However, his Army career was also short-lived – he and another recruit *"borrowed"* a car belonging to another soldier before taking it and going absent without leave during an alcohol-fuelled evening. The Army failed to see the funny side and Brian was discharged before even completing his training. He returned to the North East with no particular plans and took work both as a barman and as a mechanic at a local garage.

Brian Tevendale

Then he met Max Garvie. There is no doubt that Brian Tevendale was flattered by the attention he received from the wealthy, charismatic farmer. It also seems very likely that Garvie saw the young man as a potential sexual partner – in his predatory search for

31

different experiences, Garvie was said to have had sex with both men and women. Like Garvie, Tevendale had issues with alcohol. Unlike Garvie, Tevendale couldn't afford to indulge these issues at will, so although he didn't want to go to bed with Max, he was happy to hang out with Garvie as long as the older man kept him supplied with drink.

The two men spent increasing amounts of time together. Max Garvie took Brian Tevendale flying on a number of occasions and the young man was a frequent guest in the spare bedroom at West Cairnbeg Farm. Brian later said of this period:

> "We used to go flying and drinking together. He was a very charismatic guy, then he started drinking and popping pills and he went all to hell. He had it all and started to look for more excitement."[1]

It soon became clear just what further excitement Max Garvie was looking for. His complaints that Sheila was "frigid" were increasing but he had an idea of what he might be able to do about it – he would find her another, younger, lover and he hoped that this would re-kindle her interest in sex. And Max knew just the person would might be persuaded to fill this role. One night, when Brian Tevendale was staying at the farm, both he and Max drank a great deal of whisky. Then, after Brian had retired to the spare bedroom and was settling down to sleep, Max Garvie suddenly opened the door:

> *"He pushed Sheila into my room and locked the door. We had to sleep together. She was starkers and it was freezing cold. But she was an amazing- looking woman and I was probably quite chuffed about it all. Who wouldn't be?"*[2]

Brian Tevendale and Sheila Garvie spent that night together. She was thirty-three. He was twenty-one. In the months that followed, Tevendale spent more and more time at the farm, often spending the night with Sheila. On at least two occasions, he and Max tossed a coin to decide who would share a bed with Sheila that night. On a few occasions, all three ended up in bed together. Max was still interested in having sex with Brian, but Tevendale was interested only in Sheila. He became completely infatuated with this glamorous older woman.

Even though Max wasn't able to have sex with Brian, he was doing the next-best thing – he was having a tumultuous affair with Brian's sister Trudy, a curvaceous, green-eyed brunette who seemed to enjoy adventurous sex as much as Max Garvie did. The fact that Trudy was married didn't seem to bother any of the people involved, not even her husband, Alfred Birse, a local policeman who was a regular attendee at sex parties at West Cairnbeg. Trudy later described how, on more than one occasion, Max had taken her flying in order to demonstrate some aerial manoeuvres not covered in the syllabus for Private Pilot training. He had locked the controls to keep the light aircraft flying straight and level while he and Trudy somehow managed to have sex in the cramped cockpit of the tiny Bölkow while they cruised above the rolling hills and fields of the Mearns.

Trudy Birse

The foursome involving Trudy and Max, Brian and Sheila continued for some months until, as usual, Max became bored with the whole situation and in particular with Trudy. It was time, he told his wife, to find some new playmates. It quickly became apparent that there was a problem. Brian Tevendale, clearly not understanding the rules by which these games were played, had fallen hopelessly in love with Sheila Garvie. Sheila also claimed to be emotionally involved with her young lover and had no intention of giving him up.

Max was incensed. He might have been happy for Brian to have sex with Sheila when and where this suited him, but he was still a domineering and possessive husband who regarded his wife as his property. If he thought it was time for the affair to end, then he expected everyone else to comply. When they didn't he became violent and abusive, mainly towards Sheila.

She became even more depressed and confused. She left West Cairnbeg more than once to be with Brian Tevendale. At one point the two set up home together in Bradford, but Sheila couldn't bear to be parted from her children and she returned to the farm. She sought guidance from her mother, a local clergyman, her solicitor and even the proprietor of a local hotel with whom she was friendly. Each of them gave her the same advice – she should stick with her husband *"for the sake of the children."* It was the same thing that countless women trapped in unhappy marriages in the 1960s were told. In some ways it was understandable – even in the swinging sixties, divorce was looked upon as a failure, most often blamed upon the woman. But, in other ways, this well-meaning suggestion was a dreadful mistake.

Sheila continued to live at West Cairnbeg with Max, though she also continued to see Brian Tevendale regularly. Max's drinking meanwhile had worsened, and he was supplementing alcohol with even more drugs, making him even more unpredictable and volatile than usual. It was also rumoured that he had some financial difficulties at this time and that he was finding it increasingly problematic to finance his lavish lifestyle. By this time Sheila was also regularly taking Valium which left her feeling detached and depersonalised. Max threatened her often, once telling her that he would arrange to have her locked up in a clinic in London, but his threats failed to cut through her tranquilised haze.

Life would be so much better for everyone, Sheila sadly confided to Brian Tevendale one evening, if only Max was out of the way.

Notes

1 *Why we murdered a millionaire*, interview given by Brian Tevendale to the Daily Record, March 6th, 1999.

2 As above.

Chapter 4: Max Goes Missing

"Spends freely, is a heavy drinker and often consumes tranquillisers when drinking. Is fond of female company ... deals in pornographic material and is an active member of nudist camps ... may have gone abroad."

Police description of Max Garvie

published in the Police Gazette, June 1968.

On the 20th of May, 1968, Sheila Garvie reported that her husband was missing. She explained that she had last seen him on the night of 14th/15th May which he had spent at their home at West Cairnbeg. The next morning, he had told her that he was going on a trip. She assumed that he meant that he would be going abroad and most likely in his aircraft, though she couldn't remember if he had specifically said any of those things and he certainly hadn't told her precisely where he was going. She hadn't heard from him in the meantime and she was concerned.

Sheila Garvie in 1968

The police listened politely and entered the relevant details in the relevant places, but the truth was that they weren't too interested. This wasn't callousness or indifference: the simple fact is that when an adult goes missing, particularly an adult male, it's most often because he has chosen to do so. In many cases, the police have found themselves wasting time and resources searching for someone who isn't really missing. When this was added to Max Garvie's reputation as a philanderer, a drinker, a drug taker and a person who was behaving in increasingly erratic ways, the reaction of the police was probably entirely understandable. Beyond placing a highly unflattering description of thirty-five year old Max in the Police Gazette, a national publication in which requests for information and descriptions of wanted person are shared, very little active investigation was undertaken.

At West Cairnbeg Farm, life continued rather more quietly than it had done when Max was there. The sex parties and the nudist gatherings ended, though Brian Tevendale was a frequent visitor. Sheila seemed to her friends to be more relaxed, but her children, especially Wendy, the eldest, were devastated and worried by their father's absence. As the days for which Max had been missing turned into weeks and then months, several things were noticed. The first was that Sheila's friendship with Brian Tevendale became more public. The two were often seen out together as a couple, which caused more than a little gossip amongst friends and neighbours, especially when Sheila began to talk about a possible long-term relationship.

The second thing to become apparent was that no-one had heard from Max. For all his other failings, Max was a conscientious farmer, and to those who knew him, the idea that he would abandon West Cairnbeg without a qualm seemed very unlikely. The farm Grieve continued to oversee the day-to-day running of the farm, but he became increasingly uneasy about Max's disappearance. As did the Garvie family. If Max had vanished for a few days, or even a week or so, no-one would have been too surprised. But, three months after he had last been seen, people were beginning to question the story that Sheila had told of his leaving.

He had been seen on his way back home to West Cairnbeg on the evening of 14th May, but no-one had seen him after that. He hadn't taken any of his cars or his aircraft, his clothes were still in the house, none of his many friends had heard from him at all and most disconcertingly, there had been no attempt to access any of his money. It seemed impossible that he could have taken any large amount of money with him if he had left on a whim on 15th May and people began to question just how Max, with his expensive tastes, was managing to live without money?

Sheila's story of his disappearance, which had seemed plausible at first, began to look increasingly doubtful as time went on. The Garvie children, and particularly Wendy, were clearly suffering and Sheila asked her mother, Edith Watson, if she would move into West Cairnbeg to help look after them. Edith Watson was a woman made from the same stern stuff as her now dead husband. Religious, painfully honest and entirely upright, she can't have been unaware of the gossip in Laurencekirk about her missing son-in-law and she made it clear that she disapproved of Sheila's relationship with Brian Tevendale.

The pressure began to tell on Sheila and sometime around the middle of August 1968, she said a very strange thing to her mother: She said that she *"thought it was possible"* that Brian Tevendale might have killed Max. Her mother was devastated by this revelation, but she knew what her duty was. On 14th August Edith Watson went to the local police station in a state of distress so extreme that it bordered on physical collapse. She explained that she had reason to believe that Max Garvie was dead and that he might have been murdered by her daughter's lover. She also explained to the police that her daughter had been asking her about the effects of the tides off the coast near Stonehaven, and especially wondering what might have happened to an object which was dumped into the sea. This, said, Mrs Watson, made her wonder whether Max Garvie's body might be in the sea?

The police had obviously become aware of local unease about the disappearance, because they moved swiftly following the visit by Edith Watson. On August 14th, they arrested Sheila Garvie and Brian Tevendale on suspicion of murder. As soon as they were taken into custody, the star-cross'd lovers did what so many have done before and since – they immediately blamed each other.

Sheila Garvie gave a statement in which she claimed that, to her horror and surprise, Brian Tevendale and another man had come to West Cairnbeg Farm on the evening of 14th/15th May and had murdered Max Garvie and taken his body away. She thought they had then dumped it in the sea. Brian Tevendale however, told the police that Max Garvie had died in a bizarre accident involving Sheila and that his only involvement had been to help his lover out by disposing of the body. He took police officers a few miles down the coast, to Lauriston Castle near the village of St Cyrus where Tevendale had spent his youth.

Lauriston Castle

Lauriston Castle is a private residence and the oldest lived-in castle in the region. The day following his arrest, Tevendale led the police to a damp, dark, dank and generally unknown tunnel which ran west from the castle to nearby Lauriston Quarry. In the gleam of torches, the small party made their way along the tunnel until they reached a makeshift cairn of stones. One of the officers later told how, when they first saw the cairn, they were all startled to see a large toad sitting on top of it – in Scots folklore, the toad is a portent of impending death.

The officers carefully removed the stones from the cairn and underneath they found a rotting body. This was removed and forensic examination quickly proved that it was the mortal remains of Max Garvie. The examination of the body also showed that he had been dead for around three months and that death was due to a combination of brutal bludgeon injuries to his skull and a single gunshot wound to his neck caused by a .22" calibre bullet. Ballistic examination of the bullet proved that it had been fired from a rifle belonging to Max Garvie which was later recovered from West Cairnbeg Farm. Both Brian Tevendale and Sheila Garvie were charged with murder.

During interviews with the police, Brian Tevendale

had initially denied that another person had assisted with the disposal of the body but, confronted with Sheila Garvie's statement, he admitted that there had been another person there and that this was twenty-year old Alan Peters, a work colleague of Tevendale's. Tevendale had brought Peters to West Cairnbeg because he owned a car which was needed to move Max Garvie's body. A few days later, Alan Peters was also arrested and charged with murder.

When he was interviewed by the police, Peters claimed that the murder had been carried out by both Sheila Garvie and Brian Tevendale and that he had simply been an innocent bystander, too terrified to do anything but agree to assist with the disposal of the body.

All three were remanded in custody and a trial was scheduled for 19th November, 1968 at the High Court in Aberdeen.

Chapter 5: The Trial

The High Court of Justiciary building at Mercatgate in Aberdeen's Castle Street is a slab-fronted grey granite edifice which was designed in the late 1700s and completed in the first years of the Nineteenth Century. Under the Scottish legal system the High Court is used only for serious criminal cases such as rape and murder and each case is presided over by a single judge and a jury of fifteen people.

High Court of Justiciary, Aberdeen

Photo: AberdeenBill

The trial of Sheila Garvie, Brian Tevendale and Alan Peters was one of the most eagerly anticipated in the history of the North East. The story had everything that delights the tabloid press and its readers – a beautiful woman accused of murder, a wealthy, philandering and handsome murdered husband, a complicated web of emotional and sexual entanglements and, best of all, the titillating prospect of testimony of bizarre sexual perversions. No wonder that the pavements of Castle Street were thronged with so many curious on-lookers that the police had to erect crush barriers as the three accused were brought to the court on a damp, grey Tuesday morning on the 19th November.

The prosecution case was relatively simple: They contended that Sheila had persuaded Brian Tevendale to murder her husband in order that the pair could get married and so that Sheila could inherit Max's money and the farm and cash-in insurance policies worth more than £50,000. It was claimed that Alan Peters had assisted in both the murder and the subsequent disposal of the body.

All three accused had lodged pleas of Not Guilty and Sheila Garvie's solicitor, Lawrence Dowdall had, as required under Scottish Law, lodged notice that her defense included an intent to attack the character of the dead man. With Lord Thomson presiding as Judge and the members of the jury listening avidly, the trial got under way. And it immediately became obvious that all three accused were going to describe very different versions of what had happened on the night of May 14th/15th.

Sheila Garvie was represented in court by the flamboyant, dramatic and very able Lionel Daiches Q.C. and he carefully and gently drew out of his client her version of what happened on that night. Sheila described how she and Max had gone to bed relatively early, made love and then fallen asleep. Then, at around 11:30 P.M., she was woken by the sound of someone whispering that she should get up. Surprised and frightened, she realized that a man was standing by her bed and, by light coming from the landing outside she recognized him as her lover, Brian Tevendale. Max slept on and Tevendale led Sheila from the bed out on to the landing where she saw another man she did not recognize. Tevendale then pushed her into the bathroom and warned her to stay there. At this point she realized that he was carrying a gun. Terrified, Sheila remained in the bathroom as the sound of *"terrible thumping noises"* came from the bedroom.

Five minutes later, Tevendale returned to the bathroom and told Sheila that *"You won't have any more of him to put up with."* He instructed Sheila to stand in front of her daughter's bedroom door, in case they tried to come out while Tevendale and the other man wrapped Max's body in *"a sort of groundsheet"* and dragged it out of the bedroom, then took it downstairs and out of the house. Sheila's account made it clear that she knew nothing about the murder before it happened and that Brian Tevendale had spontaneously decided to murder Max.

Sheila went on to describe how she spent the months after Max's murder wracked by guilt and terrified of exposure. When Lionel Daiches gently asked why, in that case she had not gone to the police, her explanation was as lucid and reasoned as all her other testimony. She told the court:

> *"I felt morally responsible because I had allowed Brian to fall in love with me and had become emotionally involved with him. I felt I had unconsciously provoked him in the emotional in which he was. I was at a crossroads in my life. I took a decision that night, whatever happened, I would protect*

49

Brian because of what he had done for me."

Despite the fact that she later claimed that she had been so dosed up on tranquilisers that she felt *"out of herself"* while giving evidence, Sheila Garvie's testimony portrayed a consistent version of events. She was a woman who had been driven by the extreme behaviour of her husband to seek solace in the arms of another man. She was utterly horrified when her lover murdered her husband, but she felt morally obligated to protect him at all costs, even though this left her wracked by guilt. Her story was slightly undercut by the prosecution who provided evidence of her enjoying light-hearted fun with Tevendale in the months after the murder and even produced a photograph taken during a picnic where a laughing Sheila was seen lying underneath another man.

Brain Tevendale chose not to testify at the trial. Lacking the money to take on a team as well-known as those who defended Sheila, he was forced to rely on advocates appointed by the court. His solicitors presented a very different version of events on the night in question, essentially the same story that Tevendale had told to the police when he was first arrested. He claimed that he had arrived at West Cairnbeg Farm following an urgent, late-night summons from Sheila. When he arrived, he found her distraught and Max dead in the bed upstairs. Sheila explained that Max had insisted that she engage in a new sexual perversion, one which involved his loaded rifle. Sheila had agreed and during the ensuing calisthenics, Max had somehow and accidentally been shot and killed. Sheila begged Brian to help her get rid of Max's body, which he agreed to do.

Unsurprisingly, this story failed completely to convince the jury or anyone else in court. One principal objection was the forensic evidence – it was clear that Max had died as a result of his skull being severely fractured when he was brutally bludgeoned and before he was shot. At one point, Max Garvie's skull was produced in court to re-enforce this point, to the evident horror of Sheila Garvie and the jury. The members of the jury found a great deal of the testimony to which they listened distressing. One female juror became so upset during testimony by a clearly distraught Edith Watson that she had to be excused from the court and the jury thereafter comprised just fourteen people.

Alan Peters was also represented by court appointed advocates, but he did give testimony in his own defence. He admitted that Brian Tevendale had asked him some weeks before the murder if he would help him *"get rid of a man"*, though he also claimed (not particularly credibly) that he had not understood that this would involve murder. On the night in question, he described how the pair had gone to West Cairnbeg and Sheila Garvie had met them inside the house and taken them up to the bedroom where Max Garvie was sleeping. Brian had then smashed Max on the head with the butt of the rifle before shooting him in the head. Peters claimed to be traumatised by the murder and terrified that *"if I didn't assist in any way, I'd get the same."*

Although Peters was just twenty years old, he gave his evidence confidently and clearly and made a good impression on the jury. The problem was that what he said completely undercut the stories told by both Sheila Garvie and Brian Tevendale. The next witness would undercut these stories even further.

Trudy Birse appeared as a witness for the prosecution. She told of her affair with Max and of wild shenanigans in his aircraft, but the most significant part of her testimony concerned what Sheila Garvie and Brian Tevendale had told her. She explained that Sheila had described how Brian and Alan Peters came to West Cairnbeg on the evening of 14th/15th May and waited downstairs while she went up to check that Max was asleep. When she returned and told the two men that Max was safely asleep, all three returned to the bedroom and the murder was done. Trudy also claimed that Brian Tevendale had told her a similar story, (though in his version he claimed that Alan Peters had struck Max Garvie on the head) and that even when they were together, the two had admitted to her not just committing the murder, but that it was planned and agreed between them both beforehand.

This was significant and critical evidence. It destroyed the testimony of Sheila Garvie and was entirely different to the version of event s presented by Brian Tevendale. It was specifically highlighted in his summing-up by the Judge:

> *"If you accept Mrs Birse's evidence, there is evidence that Mrs Garvie said to Mrs Birse something to the effect that she had gone into the room upstairs and told Tevendale and Peters that Max was asleep. If that is true, it is a damning piece of evidence against her."* [1]

On the 2nd December 1968 and after ten days of listening to the evidence, the remaining fourteen members of the jury delivered their verdict. People had been queuing outside the High Court building since 3:00am in the morning in the hope of getting a seat for the final act in a trial which had been avidly followed by the press all over the UK.

The jury had not believed either Sheila Garvie or Brian Tevendale's version of events. Brian Tevendale was found guilty of murder by unanimous agreement. Sheila Garvie was also found guilty of murder, but only by a majority vote. Both were sentenced to life imprisonment.

The case against Alan Peters was found Not Proven, a verdict only available in Scotland which means that, while the jury accepts that there may be some substance to the charges, they do not believe that the prosecution has proved them beyond reasonable doubt.

Notes

1 From *Classic Scottish Murder Stories*, Chapter 14, by Molly Whittington Egan, 2011.

Chapter 6: Aftermath

Newspapers reported how Sheila Garvie and Brian Tevendale had embraced and kissed before being led away after the trial and there were rumours that the two would soon seek permission to be married in prison. But, just three months after being found guilty, Sheila wrote a terse note to Brian from her cell in Gateside Prison in Greenock which simply said:

> *"I have decided to have nothing more to do with you ever again."*

The note also instructed Tevendale, who was serving his sentence in Perth prison, to destroy all the letters which Sheila had previously sent him. Sheila never explained why she did this, but her solicitor told reporters that she had decided that the affair was *"more folly than love."*

In 1978, after serving ten years of her sentence, Sheila Garvie was released from prison on parole. For a time she ran her Aunt's guesthouse in Aberdeen and in 1979 she married a Rhodesian man, David McLellan. However, it seemed that her ability to choose men wisely had not improved and the marriage ended less than two years later in *"bitterness and violence."* In 1980 she published a book, *Marriage to Murder: My Story* in which she re-stated her contention that she had known nothing beforehand about the murder of Max Garvie. In 1981, she was married again, this time to Stonehaven man Charles Mitchell. This marriage seemed happy and he and Sheila ran a guest house in Stonehaven for a number of years. Charles Mitchell died in 1992. Sheila refused all requests for interviews and never talked about the murder. In 2015 she moved into a care home in Stonehaven.

Brian Tevendale was also released in 1978. He married and ran a bar in the village of Scone, near Perth for a number of years. In 1999, Tevendale provided a long interview to the Daily Record newspaper in which he talked in detail about the murder and his relationship with Sheila Garvie. His bitterness at what he saw as her betrayal of him is only too clear in the interview. He admitted to the killing of Max Garvie, but said that the initial idea had come from Sheila:

> *"I can't remember how she worded it, but she said it would be better with Max out of the way. I was shocked, but I'd have done anything she wanted. Having Max out of the way meant we could get married and I*

assumed that was her motive. Looking back on it now, I'm not so sure. There was a lot of money to be gained from it. And I was under her spell."[1]

His description of the murder in the same interview also clearly implicated Sheila:

"Sheila let us in through the kitchen door and took us into the sitting room for drinks. She handed me a loaded .22 rifle that Max kept in his office. After drinks, she took us upstairs to a room across the hall from their bedroom and left us there to wait. It was like a nightmare. Sheila came back and led us to where Max was lying sleeping, then stood in the doorway in case the children woke up. Max was lying on his back. I shot him in the head once. I think I put a pillow over the end of the gun to make sure there would be no sound. Then we went downstairs and scoffed a whole bottle of whisky."[2]

Tevendale also said that he was still very much in love with Sheila at the time of the trial and completely devastated when she told him that she wanted nothing further to do with him:

"I had to keep hoping we would end up together, otherwise it had all been for nothing. If I could go back and undo it now, I would. But when I did what I did, I was stupid and naive and probably thought I was in love."[3]

In 2003, while preparing for a move to live permanently in the Gambia, Brian Tevendale died of a heart attack at the age of 58. Despite the fact that they lived less than sixty miles apart after they were released from prison, he and Sheila Garvie never again met after they last saw each other in court on 2nd December 1968.

The children of Max and Sheila Garvie were looked after in the immediate aftermath of the trial by Edith Watson, Sheila's mother. One year later, she died and the children were placed with a foster family in Lanarkshire. The effect on them of the murder, the trial and all its sordid revelations must have been devastating. To lose one parent to murder is bad enough. To lose one to murder and the other to imprisonment for that murder is beyond imagining.

Wendy, the eldest child, seemed to suffer the most. She married at sixteen, less than four years after the trial. The marriage didn't last and Wendy moved to England, lost touch with her family and descended into a hell of drug and alcohol abuse and mental health issues. She has spoken several times about writing a book about the murder, partly as a form of therapy to help her deal with her feelings, but to date, this hasn't happened. Wendy had very little contact with her mother after she was released from prison and in 2002 she gave an extended interview to the Scotsman Newspaper in which she provided one damning revelation: she claimed that, when she was putting the children to bed on the evening of 14th May, Sheila had said to them *"No matter what, don't get up!"*[4] This completely undercuts Sheila's assertion that she knew nothing about the murder beforehand and strongly suggests that she knew what was planned for that night. Wendy also described in the same interview how, some weeks before the murder, she had seen her mother and Tevendale kissing passionately, but Sheila Garvie had made her promise not to tell her father.

Lloyd and Angela, the other two children of Max and Sheila Garvie, seemed to cope better with the tragedy. Angela became involved in journalism and became a senior and respected writer for a well-known women's magazine in London. West Cairnbeg remained in the Garvie family and Lloyd eventually returned to live there with his wife and family and to run the farm. He added even more new features to the already luxurious house before putting it up for sale in 2015.

The marriage of Trudy and Fred Birse was fatally damaged by the revelations which became public at the trial and they divorced in 1971. Fred was given custody of their three children and remarried. He died of cancer in 1985. Trudy never re-married and she worked as a housekeeper in Dunkeld until her death, also from cancer, in 1988.

Alan Peters was married at the time of the trial and he went on to have two children, but he and his wife divorced in 1973.

Notes

1 *Why we murdered a millionaire*, interview given by Brian Tevendale to the Daily Record, March 6th, 1999.

2 As above.

3 As above.

4 *The Sins of my mother*, article in The Scotsman newspaper, 1st February 2002.

http://www.scotsman.com/lifestyle/the-sins-of-my-mother-1-595767

Conclusion

In most murder cases, one's sympathy usually and naturally goes to the victim. That's difficult in this case. By most accounts, Max Garvie was a repellant human being who treated his wife in the most appalling manner. There is no doubt that his treatment of Sheila would now be recognized as constituting sustained and horrendous abuse. In these more enlightened times, it seems likely that this would be recognized and Sheila would be offered help and support that would have allowed her to escape from her predicament. The advice she was actually given at the time, to stick with her husband for the sake of the children, is sadly typical of what women were told in the sixties, and there is no doubt that Sheila's desperate desire to escape from her husband without losing her children was a factor in this crime.

Sheila's attempt to shift the blame for the murder entirely on to Brian Tevendale is much harder to accept. The evidence provided by Trudy Birse and Alan Peters at the trial and statements made by Wendy Garvie and others afterwards make it seem much more likely that Sheila not only knew what

Brian Tevendale planned to do, she assisted him in setting the scene even if she took no part in the actual murder. Perhaps, as he later claimed, she had also persuaded him to undertake the murder in the first place?

Sheila Garvie's knowledge beforehand of the murder is really the only mystery here. Did she know what Brian Tevendale planned to do? One of the key principles to any investigation of crime is to consider Cui Bono – *"for whose benefit?"* In other words, who stands to benefit from the crime? In this case, that's fairly clear. Brian Tevendale stood to gain only the gratitude of his lover and perhaps the opportunity to spend more time with her. Sheila Garvie stood to escape from an abusive relationship in addition to inheriting her husband's money and property, getting undisputed custody of her children and collecting some substantial insurance pay-outs. Sheila Garvie had much more to gain from the murder of Max Garvie, and perhaps that should make us suspect that she knew more about what happened than he has ever admitted?

Brian Tevendale was certainly a murderer. But, perhaps he too was a victim? In later life he came to believe that he had been manipulated by Sheila into committing the murder and then expected to shoulder all the blame and leave her in the clear. When he failed to do the latter, and to his obvious and understandable bitterness, Sheila dropped him without delay.

As in most cases of murder, there were no happy endings here. Max Garvie died, Sheila and Brian were sent to prison and everyone else involved ended up hurt or suffering in some way. To those who plan them, murders must sometimes seem like the simplest solution to their problems. They almost never are. Murders cause invisible waves of grief, suspicion, guilt, hate and anger to spread like ripples when a stone is tossed into a pond. Murders are insidious, causing damage not just to victims and perpetrators, but to everyone they touch. No matter how dreadful the problem, murder is not the solution.

I hope you enjoyed reading this book. If you did, please take a moment to leave me a review on Amazon. Your opinion matters and positive reviews help me greatly. Thank you.

I also welcome feedback from readers. If you have comments on this book or ideas for other books in the Murder World series, please send me an email at: stevemac357@gmail.com.

About the Author

Steve is a Scot who writes non-fiction on a range of topics including true crime and the paranormal. He has been interested in crime writing since he read his first true crime book, in secret, at the local library in 1971, when everyone thought he was studying for his homework. Now he doesn't have to do it in secret anymore and reads a range of work by various crime writers.

He is married with two grown-up children and currently lives in Andalucía in Spain.

Other Murder World Scotland Books

If you enjoyed this book, you may also be interested in these other Murder World Scotland Books which are also available on Amazon:

The Butler's Story: The extraordinary life and crimes of Archibald Thomson Hall

Archibald Thompson Hall was a complicated man. A bisexual born in the working-class back streets of Glasgow, he craved culture and the finer things in life. Sadly, his life hadn't equipped him with the means to obtain these so he stole them instead. He worked as a burglar, thief and con-man for many years before stumbling on a role that suited him well – he became a butler and transformed himself into the urbane, charming and imperturbable gentleman's gentleman Roy Fontaine.

Working as a butler certainly gave him opportunities to steal and embezzle from his employers, but it also led him to face arrest, conviction and prison on more than one occasion (though he became the first person to escape from one of Britain's first high-security prisons). It wasn't until 1977, when he was fifty-three, that he finally discovered his true vocation as a murderer. He committed his first murder in November 1977 and by January the following year he had killed five people and would almost certainly have gone on to kill many more if he hadn't been caught. This is the true story of a charming, charismatic, intelligent, entertaining, cold, ruthless and merciless killer and one of the most dangerous men in the annals of Scottish crime.

Death in a cold town: The Arlene Fraser case

One Morning in April 1998, attractive mother and housewife Arlene Fraser called her children's school in the town of Elgin on the Moray coast of Scotland. She wanted to know what time her son would be returning from a school trip? That was the last time that anyone had contact with Arlene. When a friend arrived at her house two hours later, she found no sign of Arlene and no-one has seen her since.

The search for Arlene Fraser became one of the biggest and longest running missing person cases ever seen in Scotland but no clue was found to indicate what had happened to her. Was she abducted and murdered on the instructions of Nat, her estranged husband as the police claimed? Did she run away to a new life, leaving her children, her home and her friends behind? Was she somehow involved in smuggling?

This book provides a detailed look at Arlene Fraser's disappearance, the trials and the legal maneuvering and appeals which followed. It also analyses the main theories of what may have happened to Arlene to assess which is the most likely.

The Vanishing: The Renee MacRae case

One November evening in 1976, Renee MacRae, the estranged wife of a millionaire Scottish businessman, set off from her luxury home in Inverness. She was going, she had told her husband, to spend the weekend with her sister in Kilmarnock and she took her three year old son Andrew with her.

Four hours later her BMW car was found burning in a remote lay-by on the A9, the main road to the south from Inverness. In the car there was no sign of Renee, Andrew or their luggage.

Police enquiries quickly discovered that Renee's real

reason for leaving Inverness was very different to the story she had told her estranged husband and discovered that her life was rather more complicated than it appeared from the outside. The search for the missing mother and son was huge and this became the longest running missing person investigation in Scottish history. Despite this, no trace of Renee or Andrew was ever found.

Officially, Renee MacRae is still missing and no-one has ever been charged with her murder or that of her son. However, over the forty years that have passed since she vanished, tantalizing clues have emerged that allow us to consider the various theories, to work out the most likely course of events that November night and to identify the person most likely to have caused the disappearance.

The face of Bible John: The search for a Scottish serial killer

Just like any other country, Scotland has its share of unsolved crimes. However, few have proved to be as enduringly fascinating as the story of the man who became known as Bible John and who killed at least three women in Glasgow in the late 1960s.

This murderer picked up each of his three known

victims at the Barrowland Ballroom in the east of the city centre. The bodies of all three women were later found dumped. All three were mothers, all had been menstruating at the time of their death and all were beaten, raped and strangled. In each case, pieces of the women's clothing vanished.

The murderer made no attempt to conceal or disguise himself and was seen by a number of witnesses at the ballroom and outside - one witness actually shared a taxi with the killer and one of his victims. Through discussions with these witnesses, a well-known artist working on behalf of the police produced a striking portrait of a man with red hair and blue/grey eyes and wearing a cold, rather supercilious expression. This portrait was widely publicized and became known as the face of Bible John. People wondered how the man could possibly avoid arrest with his likeness on the front of every major Scottish newspaper and on police posters throughout the city?

How was this be possible? The murderer frequented a busy public place and was seen with all his victims by a number of witnesses who got a good look at him. By the time of the third murder, there had been massive publicity and people were on their guard and actually looking for a potential killer. Given that, just how did this person manage to kill three times and yet still escape detection? Having killed three times, why did he stop? Did he really stop at all or did he just become more adept at hiding his crimes? Perhaps most importantly of all, did Bible John really exist at all or was he nothing more than an urban myth?

Printed in Great Britain
by Amazon

37815429R10040